Black Gumbo

The Healing of a City in Ruins
August 29, 2005

Written by Vera Squire

PublishAmerica
Baltimore

© 2009 by Vera Squire.
All rights reserved. No part of this book may be reproduced, stored in a retrieval system or transmitted in any form or by any means without the prior written permission of the publishers, except by a reviewer who may quote brief passages in a review to be printed in a newspaper, magazine or journal.

First printing

PublishAmerica has allowed this work to remain exactly as the author intended, verbatim, without editorial input.

Softcover 1-60836-123-3
PAperback 978-1-4512-5436-5
PUBLISHED BY PUBLISHAMERICA, LLLP
www.publishamerica.com
Baltimore

Printed in the United States of America

Dedication

I would like to dedicate this book to everyone who was affected by Hurricane Katrina

The Storm Has Gone

The storm has come and gone.
Now the sun peeks its face from behind the clouds,
and the rain and clouds roll out with the wind,
which gathers the muddy substance into the rocks which is called sand.
Then the rainbow creases the sky, from God who sits on high.
As a reminder to let us know, His Word still stands.

Introduction

This book, *Black Gumbo,* shows the different ways the hurricane took the city by storm. Literally. It also shows how the people, with the help of God, are triumphing over adversity. This book of poetry stands on Hope. It's a hope in the healing process that is still going on today.

New Orleans

First, I would like to describe my view of the city of New Orleans. New Orleans is best known for its fine cuisine and it is better known as a party town, where the music is the spice of life and Mardi Gras is the belle of the ball. To describe the music side of New Orleans, starting with Gospel music, I can truly say it is the rock that rocked throughout the city in harmony. Now Jazz, that mellow sound, is heard in the streets as well as clubs. The tap dancers are young people as well as old, but they are enjoyable for the crowd to see.

From the music side of New Orleans, to the flipside of New Orleans

New Orleans has a well-known football team with determination for reaching its goal.

Now, if you want to see the sights of the city, there are the streetcars and also horse-drawn carriages. (Please don't forget your camera.)

Artists line Jackson Square to showcase their artwork. Some artists even sketch the faces of willing participants.

The Beginning of 2005

In the beginning of 2005, when the year came in, so did lots of tourists, more than usual. You see, the city was beginning to grow economically and it was glowing with gleam. Lots of entertainment headlined the city. It even looked like the city had a grip on its finances. The money that was pouring in fattened the city waistline. Still, New Orleans had its ups and downs. But that never blocked the tourists' view in coming to New Orleans.

Now there you have it, a brief summary of my view of New Orleans, LA.

The Hurricane

It was a dark day for the people of New Orleans, LA on August 29, 2005, when Hurricane Katrina arrived. The warning came all the week echoing through the air waves of disbelief; because the people always believed that nothing so horrendous could ever hit the city.

The hurricane warning was coming in more frequently during the week before the 29th of August 2005. The 29th was on a Monday, and the warning intensified on Sunday. Most of the people were leaving the city frantically. Some wanted to leave but couldn't. Others decided to go to a safe place, wherever that might have been.

Now hard winds and rain began to come into the city, with fair warning, but the time to leave the city had left. After that time had expired, the people sat and wondered how they would survive this horror.

Boisterous winds and heavy rain began to pour down on the city, flooding the city streets in surrounding areas (before the breaking of the levees). In the old folks' mind, they knew that this wasn't the first time the city had to look down the belly of a whale because in 1965 there was a hurricane called Betsy. It too wreaked havoc, but not of this caliber. Yes, Hurricane Betsy had some of Hurricane Katrina's attributes, but only to a certain degree.

You see, Hurricane Betsy was a category 3 hurricane and Hurricane Katrina was a category 5, lessened to a category 4 when it reached land, according to the meteorologist.

Nevertheless, Hurricane Katrina was packing power as well as punches. As she pounded the city, the city took a beating on the chin. Regardless what hurricane blows into the city, it doesn't stop the people from coming back to rebuild. Today the city is still standing.

Black Gumbo

Black Gumbo, as unreal as it may seem,
black gumbo is now a part of history.
High stakes, orange alert danger,
who was a stranger in New Orleans
when she arrived on August 29, 2005.
Now because of this unwelcome stranger,
who shook, shaked and shimmied
her way through our streets, unauthorized,
when she came in! She came in with a vengeance!
She made more people cry. Some even died.
because of the black eyes and black skies
that left a hole in the heart of the city that once rumbled!
But to me, it's a city, I now call
Black Gumbo.
Black as the night that skims across the wild blue yonder.
Hmm…I wonder how black a night can be,
when it was day in reality.
After her hard hits, her right and left jabs,
that grabbed our attention,
I don't want to mention
how she dismantled cars and houses alike.
She even managed to turn off all the lights.
Hurricane Katrina was the name of this stranger
that stumbled into a city that once rumbled.
But to me, it's a city I now call,
Black Gumbo.

I'm the Streetcar Named Desire

(In this poem, chuckle doesn't mean to laugh. It is the sound the streetcar makes as it moves on the tracks, while the cable cords support its movement.)

I coiled through the streets of disparity,
but for the sake of clarity,
it's rare that I don't have anyone to take good care of me.
I came to my stop at the station,
only to find it had little circulation
of the crowds that once filled the streets.
I blew my horn, yet no one heard me
as I chuckled on through the street of misery.
But I'm The Streetcar Named Desire!
I chuckle on through these streets
without missing a beat,
as I come to face the harsh reality,
of a lesser crowd that once filled the streets.

Coming out of the storm, that came through the city,
Oh…! What a Pity!
After everything had settled and everything had calmed,
I still chuckled on
because I'm The Streetcar Named Desire!
I chuckle on through these streets,
without missing a beat,
as I come to face the harsh reality
of a lesser crowd that once filled the streets.

The New New Orleans

Halt! Who goes there?
Said the guard at the bridge.
It sent chills down my spine
aligned with my seat, as I sat still.
Halt! Who goes there?
He repeated again and said, "If you are going in the city,
you only can stay a few minutes."
You see, the city was still in ruins,
destined to be castrated because of its altered state,
after the hurricanes.

But wait, the people began to come back to the city.
They refused to let it go down without a fight.
They began to build their homes, jobs and even lives.
They even turned on all the lights.

The guards all left, as the city began to mend,
because the people refused to let New Orleans end.

Rescuers

One man stood in the face of devastation.
He cried out for help, as he held up his baby.
Still hurting from his loss, as many others' lives were lost
that day, from the rushing waters that poured into the city, Unannounced.
Help!!! Help us!!! Many screams were heard as well,
before the rescuers were on their way
to save them from this living hell.

Marooned

(Moved to another place, after the storm)

Displaced and feeling out of place, is
like a spaceship on a voyage of the unimaginable.
Now apt to adapt to a different way,
to be put back in place only to accommodate the where.
But in this new place and sometimes feeling out of place,
you can still find someone who cares.

What About the Children

Everyday children play and still trying to fit the pieces to the puzzle.
Puzzled by the storms, they don't complain, just only dance to the music
that they hear.
Parents and families cuddle them and keep them safe from harm.
Although still puzzled by the storms, they don't complain,
just only dance, to the music that they hear.

A Crying Shame

It's a crying shame! When crime tries to rule a city in its deplorable state. It's a crying shame! When crime is on the rise as high as the wind. It's a crying shame! When crime don't even take a back seat, no matter what storm blows into the city! It's just a crying shame.

Black Eyes Suzy

Black Eyes Suzy, her eyes were as black as the night.
shining through God's perfect light.
The smog that ramped through the city's skyline was caused by the hurricane, that turned the city upside down.
Suzy's eyes were still black as the night, as she crawled her way out of this terrible sight.

In James' Eyes

In James' eyes, he opened wide to see the stage of events and
began to capitalize on the things that remained after the hurricane.
In James' eyes, he counted his loss and paid the cost of the things
that remained after the hurricane.
In James' eyes, he found strength and gathered the things that
remained after the hurricane.
In James' eyes, he just knew, as he lifted his eyes to the One that's true
And gathered everything he had left after the hurricane.

Eyes of Bold Betty

In the eyes of Bold Betty, she had seen the rise and the fall of the city.
In the eyes of Bold Betty, she even saw the picking up of the pieces.
As bold as Betty was, she only holds to the one thing that means the most.
That one thing is Hope.

When I Was Sleeping

When I was sleeping,
you came in.
You tip-toed through my window,
with a terrible scream.

Tearing up my curtains,
I had just brought from the store,
Then you turned around and
Tore up my floor.

You saw all the damage and
stormed out the door.

Debris

The debris collects grass that grows into the structure,
that stands as a pillar of what was.
Now it insists it has a name,
when time digs its heels into the sand.
It stands firmly in place, like a statue
that stands its ground of contention.
Its name is Debris.

Shamble

Some people's lives were in a complete shamble. Shaken from the root, from where it sprouts the seed. Some families were scattered all over the place, then they were placed with unfamiliar faces, and in different places they had never seen before. Wondering minds and wondering eyes, still wondering.

Broken Pieces

Where do I begin?
When I see all the devastation,
seems like it has no end.

Where do I begin?
All of these broken pieces,
that I'm trying to mend,
only means I have to start all over,
And begin again.

The City of Hope

When you peel back the hands of time,
a time of not so long ago,
and look down into the mouth of yester-year,
all you can see is how far the city has come,
and how it looks today,
I can truly say, It's a city that stands,
on Hope.

City Lights

From right to left, and from left to right,
all you can see is the car lights.
Multitudes of traffic, bright lights that light up the city's skyline,
that line up in a row, for the show.

It coaches the people into the city,
from miles and miles they come, to dance until midnight into the city.

Louisiana

Louisiana is the only home I've ever known.
It's shape is like a boot,
that stamps its print into the deep river.
When I look ahead and begin to move forward,
I often look back on my tomorrow,
I think of a place I'll always call home.
Because, Louisiana is the only home I've ever known.

The Healing Process

The healing process starts with you,
so the city will come shining through
the night light it deposits throughout the year,
makes everyone stand up and cheer.
Get up New Orleans, a town that sleeps,
It's time to get back on your feet.

Morning Dew

Dress me God I pray,
in the clovers of your splendor,
which arrives like the morning dew.
Even like the dawn, when it breaks through
and peeks into its marvelous light.

Dress me, God I pray, from head to toe.
Shape me and mold me,
like the potter shapes the clay,
from which he makes, as he desires.

Dress me, God I pray, with your wisdom
of open collections and place it in my vessel.

Dress me, God I pray, with your whole armor,
dress me God today.

Morning Prayer

Good morning God.
Father, I would like to thank you for letting me see another day.
A day that I've never seen before. You made it like a picture that fits a frame that can only symbolize the journey ahead.
Be a shield and buckle, and protect me throughout the day.
In Jesus name I pray, Amen.

Standing on God's Word

The storm literally blew my church to pieces. This is what the minister said, as he looked back on that terrible day. The force of the winds displayed its mighty blows. The course it took disrupted my voice. But I would only be silent for a moment, because with the next breath that I took, my journey would continue. It may not have been in the same place, but whatever place it was, I stood on the word of God.

Worship God

(New Orleans Is Still Standing)

Worship the Lord, all honor and glory, belongs to Him.
Every knee must bow, and every tongue confess, that He is so
Worthy, He is worthy to be praised.

Worship God, bless His holy name.
Make a joyful noise unto the Lord all the land.

Serve the Lord with gladness, come before
His presence with singing.
Praise be to God and bless His holy name.

Catch the Spirit

Every day is a new page in life
Every sweet smell of success means
a victory without defeat.
Every bird that sings,
is a sweet sound to the ears.
Every day is like Sunday in heaven and
every Sunday is like heaven on earth.
especially when you are worshipping.

Never Give Up

When you hold your head up high,
never give up, just look to the sky.

Let the Lord set the pace,
while we rebuild your place,
and never give up on His grace.

Believe

It's critical to believe in Jesus,
who ministers belief.
Where there's prayer, there should be faith,
Faith moves God.
God's work isn't hard, when you include Him.

Stepping Stone

Now is stepping into the present,
and later is waiting on the future.
Reaching up and looking back,
distorts a matter, no matter what it is.
God's firm hand and His tight grip
holds everything in place, when we place him first.

Richer Moments

Life's richer moments are
moments you spend with God.
A rotten relationship
spoils a good friendship.
Getting to know God, means to lose yourself.

Heart to Heart

Hearing a word from the Lord keeps you strong.

The Way

Jesus is the way to real life.

The Truth

Jesus is the true remedy for everyday problems.

The Light

Through the dark days, His light is still shining.
And darkness cannot even comprehend it.

Prayer

When we pray together,
we are in agreement with the word of God.

Giving Love

We measure life, by giving love.

New Beginnings

New beginnings to some of us, still seem strange.
But this new beginning, still remains and we still
Have to obtain our composure.

Falls in Life

After a great fall in life, God can still lift you up.

All Things

God can do all things,
But it takes your faith to prove it.
When sorrow takes a hold on your life,
Just lean on God.
Sometimes we feel like we are strong enough to do it all.
In reality, not us, but God.

Big Clean Up

The big clean up took more than hands,
it took heart.

A New Sound

Brick by brick and pound by pound,
each co-operation of this new sound to rebuild the city
is a new sound, that's never ending.

I Remember When

I remember when.
I reached for the stars and caught the moon by its tail instead.
I remember when.
The sky was as blue as the river that reflected the light from the sun.
I remember when.
The air that we breathe was safe and pleasant, even for the birds
that fly high.
I remember when.
Clouds formed figuring different shapes of animals of all kinds,
to the imagination.
I remember when.
New Orleans was a kind of town, that loved to party until the sun
went down.
I remember when.
The band headed the French Quarters downtown, and the people
danced in the street, while others came to town.
But now the now has reared its head from behind the shadows of
memories.
Now I'll take my treasures of memories and put them all away.
Because now, new memories are happening today.